Revised

Exploring English 3

Workbook

Dr Usha Ram

Collins

Revised

Exploring English 3

Workbook

Usha Ram

Acknowledgements

The authors and publishers wish to acknowledge the authors listed below, and thank the following for permission to use copyright material.

Letter text from *Collins Primary Literacy, Pupil Book 3* reprinted by permission of HarperCollins Publishers, © 2008 Hazel Willard; *Collins Big Cat: Gathering in the Days* copyright © Gareth Owen 2011. Reproduced by permission of the author c/o Rogers, Coleridge & White Ltd, 20 Powis Mews, London W11 1JN; *Collins Big Cat: The Story of Ice Cream* reprinted by permission of HarperCollins Publishers, © 2005 Sue Graves.

Every effort has been made to trace copyright holders and to obtain their permission for the use of copyright material. The authors and publishers will gladly receive any information enabling them to rectify any error or omission in subsequent editions.

Illustrations

All illustrations by Sohom Bhattacharjee, Richa Kinra, Priyankar Gupta and Q2A Media Services Private Limited.

Cover: Olga_Bonitas, Evgeniya_m, Askold Romanov

Title Page: Olga_Bonitas, Evgeniya_m, Askold Romanov

Photographs

p28: Tigatelu, Tigatelu, Kristijan Hranisavljevic, Dualororuap, nyamol, Tigatelu; p49: kannsma

Published by Collins Learning
A division of HarperCollins*Publishers* India Private Limited

HarperCollins *Publishers*
A-75, Sector 57, Noida, Uttar Pradesh 201301, India
1 London Bridge Street, London SE1 9GF, United Kingdom
2 Bloor Street East, Toronto, Ontario M4W 1A8, Canada
Lvl 13, 201 Elizabeth Street (PO Box A565, NSW, 1235),
Sydney NSW 2000, Australia
195 Broadway, New York, NY 10007, USA

Browse the complete Collins catalogue at **www.collins.in**
for any queries/feedback, please write to us at
SCHOOLSUPPORT@harpercollins.co.in or call us on **0120-4044800**.

First edition 2015
Latest revised edition 2018

Reprint: 10 9

ISBN: 978-93-5277-144-8

Typesetting and page layout by Q2A Media Services Private Limited, Recto Graphics

Cover layout by Rahul Dhiman

Printed and bound in India by MicroPrints India, New Delhi

PREFACE

Revised Exploring English is a multi-skill course in English, designed for children and young people growing up in a world of global communication. It aims to develop their cognitive abilities, train them to think critically and communicate effectively in a wide variety of contexts. It adheres to the latest National Curriculum Framework. The series has been revised and updated based on detailed user feedback.

Built around salient themes, the units in the book comprise carefully selected reading texts authored by Indian and global writers. They cater to a variety of student interests and needs, motivate engagement and promote critical thinking. Through the reading of the texts, learners are expected to develop as thinking individuals who are keenly aware of the world around them – linguistically competent, cognitively able and morally responsible.

The eight-level series includes coursebooks, workbooks and literature readers for levels 3 to 8. Each level is also accompanied by a comprehensive Teacher's Resource Book and digital resources for the teacher in the form of an interactive DVD.

Workbooks 1 – 5

The workbooks are mapped to the coursebooks and are designed to complement them by providing additional material for skills practice, review and assessment. The grammar sections give a short reminder of the main grammar point covered in the corresponding unit in the coursebook, and are followed by practice exercises to reinforce the language. There are also plentiful practice exercises to practice key vocabulary, language skills, reading and writing. The workbooks also contain Activity sections and Test sections, which can be implemented in the school year.

Coursebooks

Each Coursebook comprises ten units, each of which is based around a main reading passage. Each unit includes a *Warm-up* to stimulate the learners' interest. A carefully selected reading passage acts as a starting point for all language work and discussion throughout the unit. This is followed by *Comprehension*, *Vocabulary* and *Grammar* exercises, as well as *Listening*, *Speaking*, *Writing* and *Language skills* activities. There are also five poetry sections in each book, followed by *Poetry appreciation* and an *Activity* which allows learners to explore the topic further. In addition, two *Projects* and two *Life Skills* are provided at each level.

Literature Readers

The Literature Readers teach critical appreciation of literature through short stories, folktales and fairytales, extracts from quality literature and classic novels, and poems from various eras and regions. A range of text-types is covered, with learners' attention being drawn to the genre of each piece. Literary devices are also highlighted, with a glossary of literary terms at the end of each book.

Teacher's Resource Books

The Teacher's Resource Books contain model lesson plans, photocopiable worksheets covering all the pedagogical aspects included in the Coursebooks, answer keys to all exercises, along with extra analytical activity sheets.

Digital resources

The Collins DigiSuite DVD comprises:

1. **Enhanced e-book:** includes the coursebook in digital format with additional features like audio, animated poems, pronunciation help and interactive exercises.
2. **Test generator:** an easy-to-use tool to help teachers create tests with a few clicks.
3. **Teacher resources:** includes lesson plans, answer keys, listening texts, additional worksheets, further project ideas, and extra support with assessment.

We hope that the course will foster a love for reading in young learners and provide teachers with language acquisition tools that can be used to effectively impart communication skills and equip young minds with an awareness about the world.

CONTENTS

Unit 1 The Tale of Peter Rabbit

Reading comprehension

A Read the following poem about a naughty boy.

Naughty Soham

Soham was a naughty boy
Who enjoyed breaking every toy;
He never followed any rule,
He thought that made him very cool!

His mother told him not to fight
But he always did what was not right;
'One day he will learn a lesson,'
Said his teachers in frustration!

Last Sunday he tried his trick
And he fell seriously sick;
He promised to be good since then,
And never be naughty, never again!

B Fill in the blanks with words from the poem.

1. Soham enjoyed breaking every __________.
2. Soham thought breaking rules made him __________.
3. His mother told him not to __________.
4. Soham's teacher said that one day he would learn a __________.
5. The day when Soham tried a trick was __________.
6. After the trick, Soham fell __________.

Vocabulary

A Match the nouns with their descriptions.

1. cabbage
2. lettuce
3. potato
4. peas
5. radish
6. blackberry

a. a round vegetable that is brown outside and white inside

b. small, round green seeds that grow in long cases called 'pods'

c. a large, round vegetable with green leaves that you cook

d. a small, soft purple fruit that grows on bushes

e. a small, red and white vegetable that grows in the ground

f. a round vegetable with green leaves that you eat in a salad

B Match the words with the pictures.

a. 

b. 

c. 

1. brinjal
2. carrot
3. cauliflower
4. garlic
5. lady's finger
6. tomato

d. 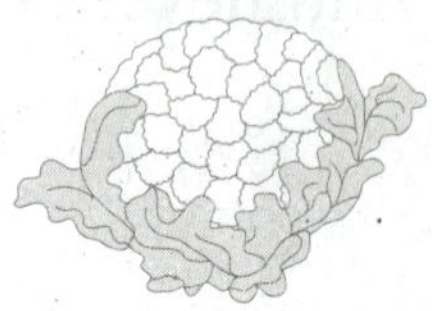

e. 

f. 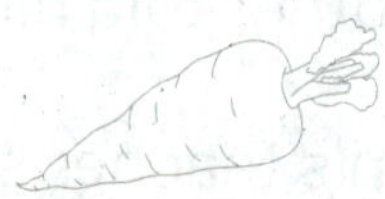

Grammar

Remember!

Common and proper nouns

- Nouns are of two types: common nouns and proper nouns.
- A **common noun** is the general name of any person, place, animal or thing.
- A **proper noun** is the special name of a person, place, animal or thing.
- A proper noun always begins with a capital letter.

  boy – common noun *Soham* – proper noun

A Write a proper noun for each of the following.

1. a book ______________________
2. a day of the week ______________________
3. a festival ______________________
4. a restaurant ______________________
5. a month ______________________

B Circle the common nouns with a red pencil and the proper nouns with a blue pencil.

1. Flopsy, Mopsy and Cotton-tail were good bunnies.
2. The Taj Mahal was built by Shah Jahan.
3. Sachin Tendulkar is a great cricketer.
4. Jaipur is a city in Rajasthan.
5. We gifted Rita a book on her birthday.
6. Ravi took his dog, Rover, for a walk.

Remember!

Countable and uncountable nouns

- We use **a** or **an** with countable nouns when there is <u>only one</u> of something.
  *Mr McGregor has **a** sieve in the garden.*
- We use **an** when the countable noun starts with a vowel sound.
  *Peter saw **an** old mouse at the doorstep.*
- We use **some** when there is <u>more than one</u> of something.
  *First he ate **some** lettuces.*
- We also use **some** with uncountable nouns.
  *He went to look for **some** parsley.*

C Fill in the blanks with *a, an* or *some*.

1. I have to do ________ work this afternoon.
2. Could you please pass me ________ pencil?
3. He lives in ________ apartment.
4. I put ________ salt in the dish.
5. My mother works in ________ office.
6. I bought Swati ________ bag for her birthday.
7. They forgot to bring ________ umbrella with them so they got wet.
8. Can you buy ________ vegetables for me, please?
9. Would you like ________ milk with the cookies?
10. He has ________ toy van.
11. I will see you in ________ hour.
12. Mum has bought ________ oranges.

Language skills

Write the plural form of the nouns under the pictures.

baby box chair lady peach tomato

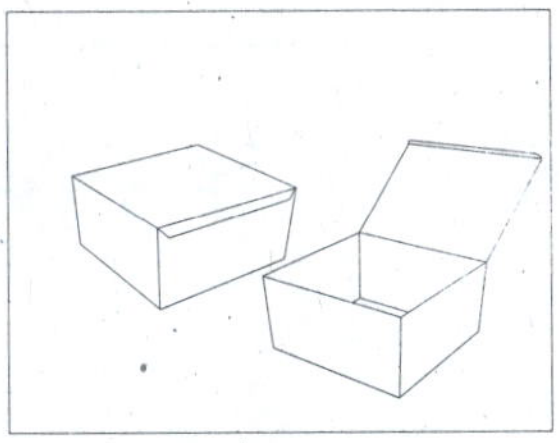

1. ____________

2. ____________

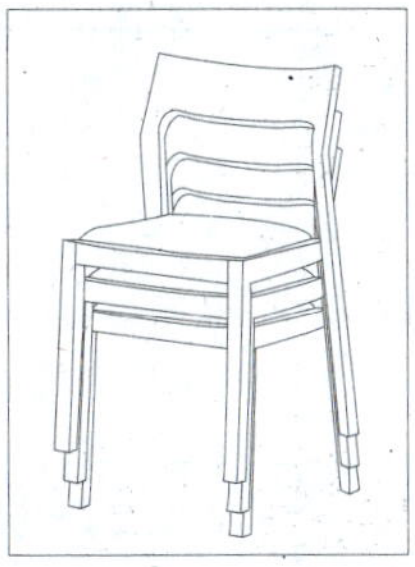

3. ____________

4. ____________

5. ____________

6. ____________

Writing

A Write five things your mother or father asked you to do last week.

My mother asked me to tidy my room.

1. ____________
2. ____________
3. ____________
4. ____________
5. ____________

B **Imagine you are at home. What can you see?**

Make lists of countable and uncountable nouns. Write the plural form of each countable noun.

Countable Nouns	Plural Form
a door	doors

Uncountable Nouns
some orange juice

Unit 2 The Emperor's New Clothes

Vocabulary

A Rearrange the letters to complete the sentences.

1. It's cold outside, Neha. Put your __________ (ACOT) on!
2. My mother put a __________ (CRAFS) around her neck.
3. You can't go outside, Maya! You haven't got any __________ (SOSHE) on your feet!
4. After school, I took off my uniform and put on a pair of __________ (SEJAN) and a t-shirt.
5. Were you wearing __________ (CSOSK) under your shoes?
6. Under his jacket, he wore a white __________ (HIRST).
7. My father looks very smart when he goes to work. He always wears a __________ (UIST).
8. When it is hot, we wear t-shirts and __________ (THORSS).
9. The children wore __________ (STOBO) on their feet when it was cold and snowy.

B Match the words with the pictures.

a. 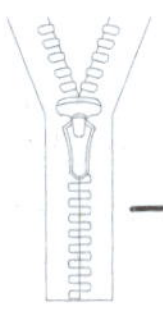

b. 

c. 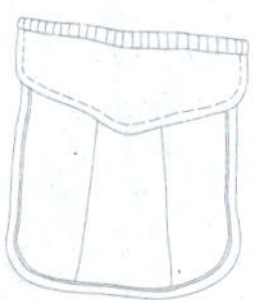

1. belt
2. button
3. collar
4. pocket
5. sleeve
6. zip

d. 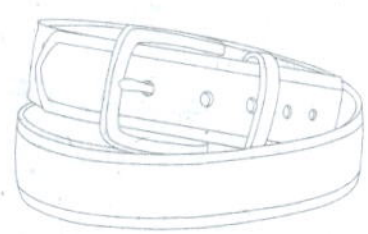

e. 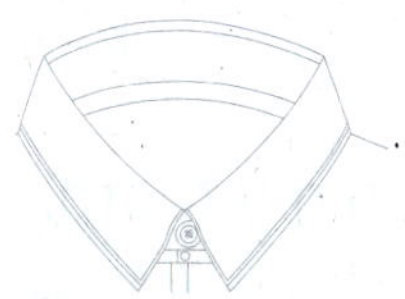

f. 

Grammar

Remember!

The simple past tense

- We use the **simple past tense** to talk about actions that were finished in the past.
- Verbs with a simple past form that ends in **-ed** are called regular verbs.

  *cook → cook**ed*** *jump → jump**ed***

  *scream → scream**ed*** *wash → wash**ed***
- Verbs which have past forms that don't end in **-ed** are called irregular verbs. You have to learn these forms one by one.

  am/is → was *are → were*

  come → came *eat → ate*

  go → went *hear → heard*

A Fill in the blanks with the simple past tense of the verbs.

brush finish help paint play rain walk want

1. I __________ my homework and went out to play.
2. Anil __________ a really beautiful picture of the mountains.
3. It's sunny today, but yesterday it __________ all day.
4. We __________ football last Saturday.
5. I cleaned my teeth, __________ my hair and left the house.
6. I __________ home from Jasbir's house.
7. I __________ my mother in the kitchen.
8. She __________ a new dress for her birthday.

B Match the beginning of each sentence with its ending.

1. I heard — a. the words out loud.
2. I wrote — b. a strange noise.
3. I came — c. a lot of vegetables.
4. I felt — d. a letter to my grandfather.
5. I ate — e. ill all evening.
6. I said — f. some nice, new clothes.
7. I wore — g. home later than usual.

Listening

Listen to Pooja talking about her weekend and write the missing words.

On Saturday morning, I [1] __________ my homework. I [2] __________ at midday and then I [3] __________ some lunch with my family. After lunch, I [4] __________ to my tennis lesson. My mother [5] __________ me there in the car. I [6] __________ two hours playing tennis and then [7] __________ home. In the evening, I [8] __________ a film on television with my brother. It was a nice day!

Speaking

Work with a partner. Choose one of these people and tell your partner which person you are. Your partner will compliment you on the clothes you are wearing.

Arjun

Pari

Sai

Sara

Writing

A Write sentences about five things you did last weekend.

Last weekend, I went for a long walk.

1. ______________________________.
2. ______________________________.
3. ______________________________.
4. ______________________________.
5. ______________________________.

B Write a list of the clothes you wore last weekend.

______________ ______________ ______________

______________ ______________ ______________

______________ ______________ ______________

Unit 3 A Pound of Butter

Vocabulary

A Choose the correct answer.

1. Who among the following is not connected to food business?
   a. baker b. cleaner c. greengrocer d. waiter
2. Which among these is not a milk product?
   a. butter b. cheese c. curd d. fried rice
3. Which among the ones given below is used to measure the weight of a thing?
   a. balance b. measuring glass c. ruler d. thermometer
4. Which of the following do we use as a unit to weigh butter?
   a. block b. degree c. litre d. pound
5. Who decides cases in a court of law?
   a. judge b. lawyer c. minister d. politician

B Add the prefix *dis-* to the words given in the box. Then, use the new words to fill in the blanks.

agreement	coloured	like	respect

1. I ________________ coffee and tea.
2. If we do not take good care of our teeth, they get ________________.
3. We should not show ________________ for the law.
4. There was a ________________ about it between the two friends.

Grammar

Remember!

Subject and object

- A sentence has a subject, a verb and often an object.
- The **subject** is usually the person or thing that performs an action.
- The **object** is a person or thing that receives an action or is affected by it.

  The police *arrested* ***the farmer***.

  Here, **The police** is the subject, **arrested** is the verb and **the farmer** is the object.

A **In the sentences given below, circle the subject and underline the object.**

1. Farmer Winston had a large farm.
2. The baker baked delicious cakes.
3. The child lost the weights.
4. Mr Carson sold a loaf of bread to Mr Winston.
5. Farmer Winston carried milk in large metal cans.
6. We must never cheat people.

Remember!

Present continuous tense

- We use the present continuous tense to talk about what is happening now.
- We form the present continuous with: subject + **am/are/is** + verb-**ing**.

  I ***am walking*** *to school.*
  He ***is learning*** *to spell.*
  We ***are going*** *to the market.*

B Complete each sentence with the correct form of the verb. Use the present continuous tense.

cry   eat   read   sing   sleep   swim

1.

He is swimming.

4.

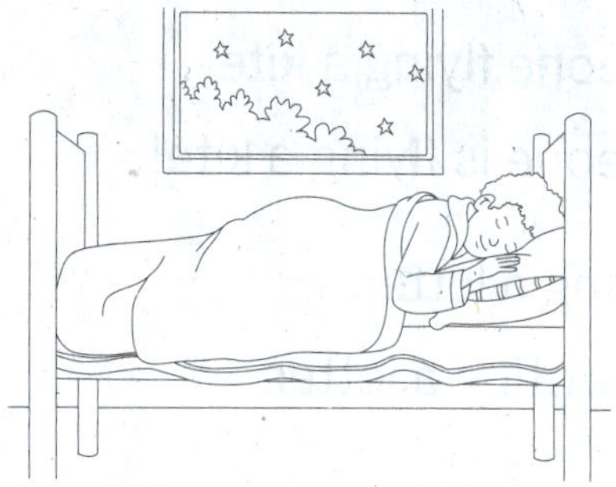

He ________________.

2.

He ________________.

5.

He ________________.

3.

He ________________.

6.

He ________________.

C **Tick (✓) the correct sentence in each pair.**

1. a. Asad is looking out of the window. ☐
   b. Asad is look out of the window. ☐
2. a. Someone flying a kite! ☐
   b. Someone is flying a kite! ☐
3. a. I writing a letter. ☐
   b. I am writing a letter. ☐
4. a. Are you watching TV at the moment? ☐
   b. Are you watch TV at the moment? ☐
5. a. Do you waiting for Vijay? ☐
   b. Are you waiting for Vijay? ☐
6. a. Where are we going? ☐
   b. Where do we going? ☐

Writing

A **Think of five people in your family. What are they doing at the moment?**

My older sister is studying for her exams.

1. ______________________________
2. ______________________________
3. ______________________________
4. ______________________________
5. ______________________________

B **What is happening in each picture? Write a few sentences using the present continuous tense.**

1.

2.

3.

Unit 4 The Magic Room

Reading comprehension

A Read this story about a turtle who was not happy with his life.

The Eagle and the Turtle

The Turtle was not happy with his life. He wanted to stop being a turtle.

'I am tired of swimming in the sea and crawling on the beach, getting nowhere in particular,' he complained. 'I want to be able to fly in the air like an eagle.'

He spoke to the Eagle about it.

'You are not made to fly,' the Eagle told the Turtle. 'You have no wings.'

'Don't worry about that,' answered the Turtle. 'I have seen how the birds do it. I don't have wings, but I can make my four flippers act like four stout[1] oars[2] in the air, the way I do in the water. And if you carry me as high as the clouds, I will bring you lots of rare pearls from the sea.'

The Eagle was greedy for the pearls, and carried the Turtle up to a great height.

'Now, then,' cried the Eagle, 'Fly!'

But the Turtle tumbled[3] from the sky. Luckily, he fell on a heap of dry grass. 'How foolish I was!' said the Turtle. 'I belong in the sea, just as the eagle belongs in the sky.'

He made his way back to the sea, and as he felt the cool water touch his skin, he said, 'I never thought I would welcome the sea so much.'

from Aesop's Fables

Wordfile

1. Something that is **stout** is thick and strong.
2. An **oar** is a long pole with a flat end which you use to make a boat move through the water.
3. If you **tumble**, you fall somewhere.

B Number the sentences in the correct order.

☐ The Eagle agreed. He carried the Turtle high into the sky.

☐ The Turtle fell, but was not hurt.

☐ The Turtle was bored with walking and swimming. He wanted to fly.

☐ The Turtle went back to the sea and was happy to be just a turtle.

☐ The Eagle dropped the Turtle. The Turtle could not fly.

☐ The Turtle asked the eagle to carry him into the sky. He promised to give the Eagle pearls from the sea.

C Answer the questions.

1. Why was the turtle unhappy with his life?

___

2. Why didn't the eagle want to help the turtle at first?

___

3. Why did the turtle think he could fly?

___

4. What happened when the turtle tried to fly?

___

5. What did the turtle think at the end of the story?

___

___

Vocabulary

A Match the synonyms (words with similar meanings).

1.	arrive	a.	alone
2.	delicious	b.	complete
3.	finish	c.	nice
4.	lonely	d.	reach
5.	pleasant	e.	steps
6.	stairs	f.	tasty

B Match the antonyms (words with the opposite meanings).

1.	wet	a.	rude
2.	safe	b.	cheap
3.	quiet	c.	alive
4.	expensive	d.	noisy
5.	dead	e.	dry
6.	polite	f.	dangerous

Grammar

Remember!

Prepositions of place and movement

- Prepositions of place describe where something is.
  The bird catcher locked the poor birds ***in*** *a cage.*
  There was a little boat – and ***on*** *it was my brother.*
- Prepositions of movement describe where someone is going.
  The diver dived ***into*** *the waves and swam.*
  The dolphin came ***out of*** *the water.*

A **Put the words in the correct order to make sentences. Remember to use capital letters and full stops.**

1. I walk/my friends/to school/with

____

2. keys behind/my father's/the sofa/we found

____

3. I/like to/on a train/sit next/to the window

____

4. bag under/put your/the desk/you usually

____

5. bed at/got into/I finally/nine o'clock

____

B **Complete the sentences with the correct prepositions.**

across   from   into   off   on   out of   through   to

1. It was a lovely hot day and we all jumped __________ the pool.
2. Someone shouted 'Fire!' so we ran __________ the building and into the street.
3. I've put some food __________ the table for you, children.
4. My father came home __________ work a little later than usual.
5. The boy fell __________ the see-saw and hurt his knee.
6. What time do you go __________ school in the morning?
7. The train went __________ the tunnel and came out the other side.
8. The children ran __________ the playground from the roundabout to the swings.

Language skills

Add capital letters and full stops to the following sentences.

1. i am shiva and i live in mumbai

____

2. my favourite film is toy story

____

3. my friend speaks english very well

____

4. we play cricket every friday

____

5. last year I went to sri lanka

____

6. we are reading pinocchio in our english lessons

____

Writing

A Fill in the blanks and complete the 'thank you' note to your best friend, who gave you a gift on your birthday.

Dear ____________,

Thank you very much for the ____________ you gave me on my ____________. It is ____________. I like it because ____________.

Love,

____

B **What are you going to do this weekend with your friends or family? Write three suggestions using *Let's, How about* and *Shall we*.**

1. ______________________________

2. ______________________________

3. ______________________________

• Unit 5 Mongoose Becomes King

Vocabulary

A Name the animals given below.

duck   fish   frog   mare   penguin   turtle

1. 

____

4. 

____

2. 

____

5. 

____

3. 

____

6. 

____

B Rearrange the letters to complete the sentences.

1. My little sister is really _______________ (DASCER) of spiders. She runs away when she sees one!

2. I didn't want to go in the water, but I knew I had to _______________ (CEFA) my fears, so I just jumped in.

3. I was so scared before I jumped – I was __________ (SHIKANG) with fear.

4. I didn't like talking before people when I was younger, but I'm much more __________ (NOCFEDINT) now.

5. A huge dog suddenly ran up to me. I was so scared, I __________ (FREOZ) – I just couldn't move.

6. My cousin tried to __________ (RESAC) me by telling me there was a lion in the park.

Grammar

Remember!

Pronouns

- Pronouns are words that we use in place of nouns so that we do not repeat a noun or a name.

  Ravi wants to buy a pen. ***He*** *goes to the market.*

- The words **he**, **she**, **it**, **they**, **you**, **I** and **we** are all pronouns.

  The animals came together for a meeting. ***They*** *were watching the sun set.*

  The mongoose was holding ground! ***He*** *did not move an inch.*

A Underline the correct word to complete the sentences.

1. Bela and I went to Mandip's party and *they/we* had a great time.

2. Nishi gave me some cake but *I/me* didn't like it.

3. Sara and Ayesha got home very late and *they/we* were very tired the next morning.

4. Yusuf didn't understand and *he/she* asked the teacher to explain.

5. Mira was upset and *he/she* started to cry.

6. I have a tennis racket but *he/it* is quite old.

7. My mum wanted to make a cake so *her/she* bought all the ingredients.

8. My brothers are very good at football and *them/they* play every evening.

B Match the beginning of each sentence with its ending.

1. It's Farida's birthday today and	a. they have invited me!
2. Amir is leaving today and	b. she is very excited.
3. Avneet and Gopa are having a party and	c. we can't decide which film to see.
4. I have a beautiful little bird at home, but	d. they are studying hard.
5. My mother and I want to go to the cinema, but	e. he wants to say goodbye.
6. My cousins are taking their exams next week so	f. it is not very friendly.

Listening

Listen to Saba talking about something that happened to her one night. Are the sentences true or false? Circle T or F.

1. Saba is not afraid of the dark. T/F
2. Saba has a lamp next to her bed. T/F
3. Last week, a loud noise woke Saba up. T/F
4. Saba faced her fear and went to find out what the noise was. T/F
5. Saba does not know what caused the loud noise. T/F
6. Saba's little brother fell out of his bed. T/F

7. Saba's mother also woke up. T/F

8. Saba's sister went back to sleep. T/F

Speaking

Work with a partner.

A lot of people are afraid of something. Often, people are scared of things that cannot hurt them, for example, little insects. Tell your partner about someone you know who is afraid of something. What happens when they see the thing they are scared of?

> My little sister is really scared of worms. When she sees a worm on the ground, she screams and runs away.

Writing

Answer the questions. Use complete sentences.

1. What are you scared of?

____

2. Why are you scared of this thing/these things?

____

____

3. What do you do when you see the thing/things you are scared of?

____

____

4. Do you like scary stories? Why/Why not?

____

____

Activity 1

Listening

A Listen and circle the correct number of syllables.

1.	2	3	4	6.	2	3	4
2.	2	3	4	7.	2	3	4
3.	2	3	4	8.	2	3	4
4.	2	3	4	9.	2	3	4
5.	2	3	4	10.	2	3	4

B What are the children's favourite stories? Listen and match the children to the correct stories.

1. Lopa
2. Arjun
3. Sanjita
4. Manik

a. A Pound of Butter
b. The Emperor's New Clothes
c. The Tale of Peter Rabbit
d. Mongoose Becomes King

Speaking

A Read the words and say words that have the opposite meaning.

1. empty
2. friendly
3. kind
4. naughty
5. poor
6. safe
7. smooth
8. soft

B **Look at the pictures and answer your teacher's questions.**

Teacher's questions

What is this? (*point to cloud, tree, bird, butterfly, rabbit, river, plant/flower, grass, sun*)

What is the weather like in each picture?

Where are the rabbits? What are they doing? Why?

Where are the birds? What are they doing?

Which picture do you like more? Why?

Test 1

Total marks: 60
Time: 2 hours

Reading comprehension

15 marks

A Read this letter from Danny to his friend, Sam.

16 Kensington Drive,
Morwick Green,
West Yorks.

7th April

Dear Sam,

I hope you're enjoying the holiday and everyone is well.

Yesterday, we had a wonderful trip to the National Museum of Photography, Film and Television in Bradford. They have an enormous cinema screen for special films, called IMAX. When I say enormous, I mean ENORMOUS! It's three storeys high, and when you're watching a film, you can turn your head to look up, down and sideways.

We saw a film called *The Grand Canyon*. It was like being there. Did you know that the Grand Canyon is in the USA? It is a long, deep valley with steep sides made of rock. The different types of rock in the canyon tell us a lot about how our planet was formed. We were at the bottom of the canyon and you could look up and see the canyon rim high above you. It was incredible! You really must come over soon and I'll take you (to the museum, not the Grand Canyon!).

That's all I've got time for now. Dad says I must tidy up my room. I suppose that means pushing more stuff under the bed!

See you soon!

Your friend,

Danny

B Choose the correct answer. **6 × 1 = 6 marks**

1. Where did Danny go yesterday?
   a. on holiday
   b. to a museum
   c. to the Grand Canyon
   d. none of these
2. What is in the National Museum of Photography, Film and Television?
   a. a really big cinema screen
   b. a very big valley
   c. different types of rock
   d. none of these
3. Where is the Grand Canyon?
   a. in Bradford, UK
   b. in the museum
   c. in the USA
   d. none of these
4. What can we learn from the different types of rock in the Grand Canyon?
   a. how films are made
   b. how old our planet is
   c. how planet Earth was formed
   d. none of these
5. How do you think Danny felt about the film?
   a. He thought that it was amazing.
   b. He thought that it was OK.
   c. It wasn't very interesting for him.
   d. none of these
6. What do we learn about Danny from the end of his letter?
   a. He doesn't like tidying his room.
   b. He is good at tidying up.
   c. He is a very tidy person.
   d. none of these

C Answer the following questions. **2 × 4½ = 9 marks**

1. From where has Danny written the letter to Sam? What's the relation between Danny and Sam?

   ____

   ____

2. Describe the enormous cinema screen, mentioned in the letter, in your own words.

   ____

   ____

Coursebook comprehension

15 marks

A Are the sentences true or false? Circle T or F. **7 × 1 = 7 marks**

1. In 'The Tale of Peter Rabbit', Peter disobeys his mother by going where she says he must not go. T/F
2. In 'The Emperor's New Clothes', two weavers visit the city and weave the most beautiful clothes for the Emperor. T/F
3. In 'The Gymnastic Clock', the child exercises every morning. T/F
4. In the story 'A Pound of Butter', Farmer Winston proved to be a cheat. T/F
5. In the story 'The Magic Room', Poppy met the genie in the attic. T/F
6. In 'I Met a Dragon Face to Face', the child meets a dragon in real life. T/F
7. In 'Mongoose Becomes King', all the animals were afraid of the mongoose. T/F

B Match the sentence parts to form meaningful sentences. **8 × 1 = 8 marks**

1. Flopsy, Mopsy and Cotton-tail	a. a genie in the strange room.
2. The emperor spent	b. a good baker.
3. The little clock	c. a lot of money on his clothes.
4. Mr Carson was	d. through his books.
5. Poppy saw	e. reminds the child to exercise.
6. The mongoose knew that	f. got wet in the rain.
7. The poet went on many adventures at the age of ten	g. we should look fear in the face and never run from our fears.

Grammar

15 marks

A Write the plural form of the nouns. **4 × 1 = 4 marks**

1. blackberry ____________
2. fox ____________
3. peach ____________
4. potato ____________

B Write the simple past tense of these verbs. **3 × 1 = 3 marks**

1. ask ____________
2. dance ____________
3. stare ____________

C Answer the questions. Follow the instructions in the brackets.
8 × 1 = 8 marks

1. I'm afraid I can't come out to play with you. I ________________ (do) my English homework.

   (Fill in the blank with the present continuous form of the verb in brackets.)

2. I come home ________________ school at four o'clock.

   (Fill in the blank with the correct preposition.)

3. My brother and I play cricket every day after school. *They/We* love it!

   (Choose the correct pronoun.)

4. Mummy asked me to buy ________________ bread.

   (Fill in the blank with 'a', 'an' *or* 'some'.*)*

5. For this recipe you need ________________ carrot and ________________ onion.

   (Fill the blanks with 'a', 'an' *or* 'some'.*)*

6. I ________________ (decide) to call Neera and ask her.

   (Fill in the blank with the simple past form of the verb in brackets.)

7. I cleaned my teeth and ________________ (ask/brush/dance) my hair.

   (Fill in the blank with the simple past form of one of the verbs in brackets.)

8. Sara and Mira were in the drawing room. She was watching TV.

   (Correct the error in this sentence.)

Writing

15 marks

A **Write about what you did at the weekend. Use the simple past tense. You may use these or any other verbs.** **8 marks**

buy	cook	draw	eat	go	paint	play
read	visit	walk	watch	work	write	get up

B **Imagine you had a magic wand. Write what you would do with it. You can use the following phrases in your writing.** **7 marks**

all English words — excellent grades in all subjects — toys and chocolates — a lot of money — poor people

Unit 6 Abdullah and his Greed

Reading comprehension

A **Read this poem about memories and try to imagine the moments the poet describes.**

Gathering in the Days

I saw my grandad late last evening
on a hillside scything[1] hay
Wiped his brow gazed about him
Gathering in the day.

My grandmother beside the fireplace
Sleeps the afternoons away
Wakes and stirs the dying embers[2]
Gathering in the day.

Heard screams of laughter from the orchard
Saw a boy and girl at play
Watched them turn their heads towards me
Gathering in the day.

And my mother at a window
On some long-forgotten May
Lifts her eyes and smiles upon us
Gathering in the day.

And all the people I remember
Stopped their lives and glanced my way
Shared the selfsame[3] sun an instant
Gathering in the day.

Gareth Owen

Wordfile

1. If someone **scythes** a crop, they cut it using a tool with a long, curved blade.
2. The **dying embers** of a fire are the pieces of wood, etc. that are still hot when a fire has stopped burning.
3. **Selfsame** is another way of saying 'the same'.

B Answer the questions.

1. The poet writes about short moments that he remembers from the past. Which people does he remember?

____

____

2. What is the poet's memory of his grandmother? Why do you think he remembers her this way?

____

____

3. How does the poet remember his mother? What does this suggest about his mother?

____

____

4. At the end of the poem, the poet mentions the sun. What does he say about it?

____

____

5. Find the words from the poem which mean:

   a. to collect something together _______________

   b. to look at something or someone for a long time _______________

Vocabulary

A Fill in the blanks with the correct verbs.

gather   gaze   glance   share   stir   wipe

1. If you __________ something, you move your hand or a cloth across it, often to make it dry.
2. If you __________ many things together, you get them from different places.
3. If you __________ something with other people, you divide what you have with them.
4. If you __________ at something, you look at it for a long time.
5. If you __________ at something, you look at it for a very short time.
6. If you __________ something, you move it around with a stick, a spoon or another tool.

B Match the words to form compound words.

1. book	a. bag
2. break	b. berry
3. dragon	c. cake
4. finger	d. end
5. pan	e. fast
6. straw	f. fly
7. tea	g. print
8. week	h. store

Grammar

Remember!

can, can't, must and _must not_

- We use **can** to say what is possible. (= We are able to do it.)
  *Cats **can** climb trees.*
- We use **can't** to say what is not possible. (= We are not able to do it.)
  *Dogs **can't** climb trees.*
- We use **must** to say what we have to do. (= It is something that is necessary.)
  *We **must** keep our room clean.*
- We use **must not** or **mustn't** to say what we are not allowed to do.
  (= It is important that we do not do it.)
  *We **must not** waste water.*

A Put the words in the correct order to make sentences. Remember to use capital letters and full stops.

1. a secret/so you must not/tell anyone/this is

   ____

2. help you/homework/I can/with your

   ____

3. I've hurt/my leg/run/so I can't

   ____

4. eat/something before/you go/you must

   ____

5. is sleeping/make a noise/so you mustn't/your sister

   ____

Remember!

Prepositions of time

- Prepositions of time are words that tell us when something happens. They are **in**, **on**, **at**, **until**, **during**, **after** and **before**.
- We use **in** for periods like months and years, **on** for days and dates and **at** for times.

B Fill in the blanks with *in, on* or *at*. You may use some words more than once.

1. The train will arrive _____ 3:00 p.m. It travels forty kilometers _____ two hours.
2. Sam goes to church _____ Sundays.
3. We started our journey _____ six _____ the morning.
4. I was born _____ 2 August _____ the year 2010.
5. Tomorrow _____ this time, we shall be in Delhi.
6. I wake up _____ six o'clock _____ weekdays, but at eight o'clock _____ weekends.

Writing

A Write six rules about your school, using *must* and *must not*.

We must not speak when the teacher is speaking.

1. We must ____________________.
2. We must not ____________________.
3. We must ____________________.
4. We must not ____________________.
5. We must ____________________.
6. We must not ____________________.

B **Design a poster about the rules for a holiday camp for children. Use *must* and *must not*. You can draw pictures to illustrate the rules.**

Unit 7 The Adventures of Sindbad the Sailor

Vocabulary

Circle the correct word to complete each sentence.

1. There was a terrible storm at sea and the boat *drowned/sank*.
2. Deep in the cave, they found great piles of *treasure/voyage*.
3. Later that year, the men set off on *an island/a voyage* around the world.
4. The *captain/merchant* sailed the boat across the vast sea.
5. The men *drowned/sailed* across the sea in a huge ship.
6. The men got off the boat and started to *explore/sail* the island.
7. Sadly, the boat sank and the sailors all *drowned/explored*.
8. Sindbad reached an *island/voyage* and was helped by the people.

Grammar

Remember!

The comparative form

- When we compare people or things, we add **-er** to an adjective. This form of the adjective is called the **comparative** form.

  Before the journey, Sindbad was ***rich****.*
  (= He had a lot of money.)
  After the journey, Sindbad was ***richer than*** *before.*
  (= He had even more money.)

A **Complete the sentences with the comparative form of these adjectives.**

brave	fast	high	kind	long	short

1. Anamika is a very good runner, but Tara is even __________.
2. There are two mountains, but one is much __________ than the other.
3. My sister is four years younger so she's a lot __________ than me.
4. I prefer our new teacher. I think she's __________ than our last teacher.
5. The road to your house is __________ than the road to my house.
6. I was too afraid to ask the question, but Farida was __________ than me.

B **Write the comparative form of these adjectives.**

1. cheap __________	5. safe __________
2. close __________	6. slow __________
3. fine __________	7. warm __________
4. late __________	8. weak __________

C **Match the beginning of each sentence with its ending.**

1. I've washed the car and now it's much	a. three years older.
2. I was only five at the time, but now I'm	b. newer.
3. I asked Rakesh to carry the boxes because he is	c. stronger than me.
4. My bag is quite old now. Yours is much	d. richer.
5. Ajit was quite poor, but his brother was much	e. a bit colder.
6. It was warm yesterday, but today is	f. cleaner.

Language skills

Tick (✓) the correct sentence from each pair.

1. a. I could hear the sounds of birds singing. ☐
   b. I could here the sounds of birds singing. ☐
2. a. We went swimming in the see. ☐
   b. We went swimming in the sea. ☐
3. a. I asked my mother to sew a button on my shirt. ☐
   b. I asked my mother to so a button on my shirt. ☐
4. a. The men rode past us on their horses. ☐
   b. The men road past us on their horses. ☐
5. a. We had to weight half an hour for the train. ☐
   b. We had to wait half an hour for the train. ☐
6. a. Is that a knew skirt you are wearing, Neena? ☐
   b. Is that a new skirt you are wearing, Neena? ☐

Writing

A **Make five predictions about the future for your family. Use *will*.**

My sister will be a doctor.

1. ______________________________

2. ______________________________

3. ______________________________

4. ______________________________

5. ______________________________

B **Write five sentences about your plans for this evening. Use *going to*.**

I am going to finish my English homework.

1. ______

2. ______

3. ______

4. ______

5. ______

C **Write a few sentences that show comparison between things or people. You can use the adjectives given below.**

big cheap fast hard poor rich small smart weak

Unit 8 The Three Butterflies

Vocabulary

A Underline the correct word to complete each sentence.

1. Gopa always looks after the younger children. She's very kind and *caring/furious*.
2. My father was very, very angry. In fact, I have never seen him so *calm/furious*.
3. There was nothing special about the food. It was very *jealous/ordinary*.
4. If my mother hugs me and doesn't hug my little sister, my sister gets very *jealous/loyal*.
5. Asad never thinks about other people. He's very *caring/selfish*.
6. Rakesh never says anything bad about his friends, Yusuf or Vijay. He's very *jealous/loyal* to them.

B Look at the picture and answer the following questions.

Ron Tina Sunil Anne Ali Bonny Leena Sara

1. Starting from Ron, who is in the fourth place? ____________
2. What is Leena's position? ____________
3. Who is in the second position? ____________
4. Who is the last in the line? ____________

5. What is Ron's position? __________

6. What is the position of Sunil? __________

7. Who is in the fifth position? __________

Grammar

Remember!

and, but, or

- We use **and** to join similar ideas together.
  *Individually you are just ordinary butterflies, weak **and** fragile.*
- We use **but** to show an opposite idea.
  *The Gulmohar tree offered his help to Lali, **but** he did not help Peeli and Neeli.*
- We use **or** to show that we have a choice.
  *Shall we sit under the Gulmohar tree **or** the Kachnar tree?*

A Complete the sentences with *and*, *but* or *or*.

1. There were boys __________ girls at the party.
2. I liked the samosas and the dal, __________ I didn't like the biryani.
3. There are two really good things about our teacher. She is calm __________ very kind.
4. We could go swimming __________ we could go to the cinema. We can't do both.
5. I would love to come to the cinema, __________ I can't as I have too much homework!
6. Which would you rather do: watch television __________ do some drawing?
7. I tried to call him, __________ he didn't answer his phone.

B **Put the words in the correct order to make sentences. Remember to use capital letters and full stops.**

1. and Rakesh to/come to/I asked Anil/the party

   ____

2. but/is really good/is very expensive/that café/their ice cream

   ____

3. at 8:30/at 6:30 or/see the film/we could

   ____

4. Bela is/ big eyes/long hair and/tall with

   ____

5. get/the bus/walk there or/you could

   ____

6. but forgot/I finished/my homework/my notebook/to bring

   ____

Listening

Listen to Raghav talking about a typical evening in his house. Write the missing words.

When we get [1] __________ from school, we usually [2] __________ our clothes and play outdoors for a while. Then we [3] __________ and start our homework. My brother is three years younger than me so I try to [4] __________ him with his homework. Sometimes I need a little help and my mother [5] __________ with me and helps me. My mother is usually preparing the evening meal at this point so she is quite [6] __________. If we don't have too much homework to do, we often help her in the [7] __________. We peel the vegetables, for example. We always help with the [8] __________ after the meal.

Speaking

Work with a partner. One of you can choose any of the given situations and ask their partner politely for help. The other person can politely agree to help and ask for any information they need.

> I need to ask you for a favour. Could you ... , please?

> Yes, of course. How can I help?

1. You need your glasses to read your English book, but cannot find them.
2. You need to wrap a friend's birthday present, but do not have enough time to do it.
3. You need to borrow a tennis racket because you want to play tennis with your friend.

Writing

Write a short paragraph about someone that you like very much. Describe their character using the adjectives that you have learnt in this unit and any others that you know.

My best friend, Maya, is very kind and very caring. She is always calm and she never gets angry. She is cheerful and always smiling.

Unit 9 The Red Flower

Reading comprehension

A **Read the following passage carefully.**

Once upon a time, there lived a king. He had a beautiful daughter, but she did not know how to laugh. The king was worried. He called many doctors, but they could not make the princess laugh.

The princess had friends, who would try to make her laugh. She enjoyed playing with them and listening to their jokes, but she would not laugh.

One day, her friends thought of an idea. When they next met the princess, they started to cry for every funny thing that they said. The princess was surprised. She realised how annoying it was when others did not laugh. She decided to make her friends happy and laughed out loud. Everyone was very happy and laughed with her.

B **Fill in the blanks.**

1. The princess never __________.
2. The king was __________.
3. The king called __________ __________ to make his daughter laugh.
4. The friends of the princess would tell her __________.
5. The princess __________ playing with her friends but she did not laugh.
6. One day, her friends planned to __________ for every __________ thing.
7. The princess was __________.
8. She realised it was __________ when others did not laugh.

Vocabulary

A **Complete the sentences with the correct word or phrase.**

allergic   coughing   dentist   fever
fracture   sore throat

1. Sanam can barely talk as she has a ____________.
2. Please give Raman some water as he is constantly ____________.
3. Ravi's body is burning with high ____________.
4. Tarun does not eat eggs because he is ____________ to it.
5. Arun had a ____________ in his arm bone and had to wear a sling.
6. Lila will go to the ____________ as she has a terrible toothache.

B **We go to different doctors for the treatment of different diseases. Match the different doctors with their jobs. You can use a dictionary.**

Doctor	What he/she does
1. cardiologist	a. treats skin diseases
2. dermatologist	b. treats children's diseases
3. opthalmologist	c. performs surgery
4. paediatrician	d. specialises in using X-rays
5. radiologist	e. treats eye diseases
6. surgeon	f. treats heart diseases

Grammar

Remember!

Adverbs of manner

- Words that describe *how* something happens are called **adverbs of manner**.
- We form adverbs of manner by adding -**ly** to an adjective.

bright → brightly	*The sun shines **brightly**.*
glad → gladly	*The Cock **gladly** helped the Red Flower.*
loud → loudly	*The Cock crowed **loudly**.*

A Rearrange the letters to make adverbs and complete the sentences.

1. Nishi always speaks __________ (LYLTEPIO) to her parents.
2. Shout __________ (OULDYL) so that everyone can hear you.
3. Make sure you are sitting __________ (LYFORCOMTAB) before we begin the story.
4. She locked all the doors very __________ (FULRECALY).
5. Fatima did her homework very __________ (LYKCIUQ).

B Circle the best word to complete each sentence.

1. Mini is so good at the piano! She plays *badly/brilliantly/quietly*.
2. My brother drives very fast and he's not very careful. He drives *dangerously/safely/strangely*.
3. Yusuf got 50 out of 50 in his test. He answered all the questions *correctly/pleasantly/quickly*.
4. I can't understand you. Please could you speak more *correctly/quickly/slowly*?
5. I like my neighbour. She always speaks to me *interestingly/pleasantly/softly*.

Language skills

Is the punctuation in the sentences correct (C) or wrong (W)? Circle C or W and correct the sentences that are wrong.

1. Be careful? The sea is very dangerous here. C/W

   ____

2. For lunch I had rice, dal and vegetables. C/W

   ____

3. Where do you live. C/W

   ____

4. Make sure you bring pens, pencils and paper. C/W

   ____

5. Do you all have your coats, bags and notebooks? C/W

   ____

6. Stop. Why are you going in there. C/W

   ____

Writing

A Write the names of three birds you know. Then, write some notes about each one.

seagull: white feathers, lives by the sea, eats fish

1. ______________________________
2. ______________________________
3. ______________________________

B **Now draw a picture of each bird from Exercise A and write a description of each one using your notes.**

1. ______________________________

____

____

____

____

____

2. ______________________________

____

____

____

____

____

3. ______________________________

____

____

____

____

____

Unit 10 Who did Patrick's Homework?

Vocabulary

A Tick (✓) the words that are school subjects.

1. books ☐
2. countries ☐
3. English ☐
4. geography ☐
5. Hindi ☐
6. history ☐
7. homework ☐
8. maths ☐
9. playing ☐
10. science ☐
11. social studies ☐
12. writing ☐

B Homophones are words which have the same sound but different spellings and meanings, for example, *see* and *sea*; *to, too* and *two*.
Write the correct word for each clue.

1. This beautiful thing grows on plants ____________
2. We use this to make *rotis* and bread ____________
3. A male child ____________
4. Our source of heat and light ____________
5. It grows on your head ____________
6. A rabbit-like animal ____________
7. A story ____________
8. A long flexible part of a monkey's body ____________

Grammar

Remember!

The imperative

- We use the imperative to give an order or command.

  Close the windows.
  Clean your room.

- We can make commands more polite by adding **please** or **don't forget to**.

  ***Please** close the windows.*
  ***Don't forget to** clean your room.*

A **Put the words in the correct order to make commands. Remember to use capital letters and full stops.**

1. don't/face/forget to/wash your

   ____

2. down and/sit/start/your work

   ____

3. a glass/me/of water/please bring

   ____

4. clean/don't/forget to/your teeth

   ____

5. cupboard/in the/please put/your toys

   ____

6. books at/open/page 13/your

   ____

Remember!

Order of adjectives

Sometimes, we use two or more adjectives to describe someone or something. In such cases, these adjectives should follow an order.

Number	Opinion	Size	Shape	Colour	Material	Noun
one	beautiful	small	square	green	jade	teapot
three	cute	little		gray		dogs
many	expensive			brown	leather	purses
several		large	round		glass	bowls

B **Tick the correct order of adjectives to describe the nouns.**

1. He was wearing a ____________, ____________, ____________ sweater.
   a. woollen, green, large   b. large, green, woollen
2. Lucy wore ____________, ____________, ____________ shoes.
   a. leather, brown, small   b. small, brown , leather
3. My mother has a ____________, ____________, ____________ bag.
   a. lovely, round, silk   b. round, silk, lovely
4. I bought some ____________, ____________, ____________ chocolates for my brother.
   a. tasty, big, strawberry   b. strawberry, tasty, big

Listening

Listen to Zoya talking about her school. Tick (✓) the correct answers.

1. Does Zoya go to school in her village? Yes ☐ No ☐
2. Does Zoya have a science lesson today? Yes ☐ No ☐
3. Does Zoya think that English grammar is easy? Yes ☐ No ☐
4. Is Zoya's class doing division in maths? Yes ☐ No ☐
5. Does Zoya's friend think that fractions are difficult? Yes ☐ No ☐
6. Does Zoya do her homework after her evening meal? Yes ☐ No ☐

Speaking

Work with a partner. Take turns to make polite commands.

book/desk/put

help/homework

1. coat/take off
2. open/window
3. cup of tea/make
4. tidy/your bedroom
5. hands/wash
6. coat/put on
7. quietly/talk
8. pass/the book

Writing

A **Imagine you have a robot at home. The robot can do many things for you. Write some commands for the robot. (Use imperatives.)**

B **Now draw your robot and describe it in a few sentences.**

Activity 2

Listening

A **Listen and write the words you hear.**

1. ____________
2. ____________
3. ____________
4. ____________
5. ____________
6. ____________
7. ____________
8. ____________
9. ____________
10. ____________
11. BONUS: ____________

B **Listen, colour and draw.**

Speaking

A **Look at the pictures and talk about them. Answer your teacher's questions.**

Teacher's questions

What can you see in this picture?

What is happening? How did this happen?

What is this person doing? Why do you think he/she is doing that?

What do you think is going to happen next?

These are book covers. Can you think of a title for each book?

Which book cover do you like best? Why?

B **Colour the butterfly on the left. Then work with a partner. Take turns to describe your butterflies and colour in his/her butterfly on the right.**

My butterfly

My partner's butterfly

Test 2

Total marks: 60
Time: 2 hours

Reading comprehension

15 marks

A Read about ice cream and its history.

The Story of Ice Cream

Ice cream is made from milk products – milk, cream, yoghurt or custard, and sugar. Then flavours like strawberry, chocolate or vanilla are mixed in. Special ingredients are added to keep the ice cream fresh and easy to serve. Then it is frozen.

The first ice cream was made in China more than 3,000 years ago. It was made by mixing ice with milk and sugar.

A merchant from Italy, Marco Polo, travelled across China between 1271 and 1275. He discovered the secret of ice cream and took it back with him to Italy.

It is said that Emperor Akbar was so fond of ice cream that big blocks of ice were carried from Kashmir to Delhi every day to make ice cream for him.

Ice cream was first served in England in 1672 at a banquet held by King Charles II. The King did not want to share it with most of the guests!

In 1843, the first hand-operated freezer was invented in America by Mrs Nancy Johnson. Now ice cream could be made very quickly.

Nobody really knows who invented the ice cream cone, but it appeared around the end of the nineteenth century.

Ice cream has come a long way. Who can imagine summers now without ice cream?

Sue Graves

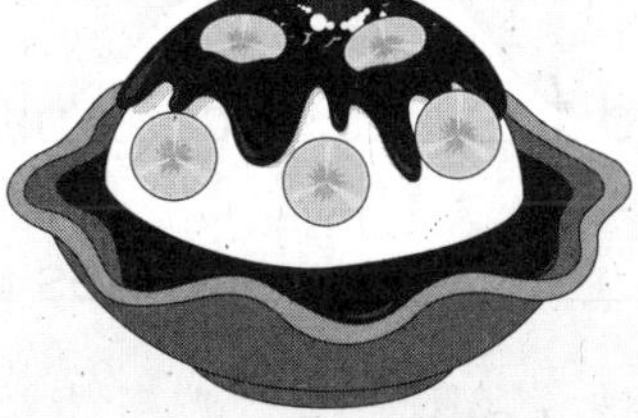

B **Answer the questions in one sentence in your notebook.** **6 x 1 = 6 marks**

1. Where was the first ice cream made?
2. How long ago was the first ice cream made?
3. What were the ingredients used to make the first ice cream?
4. Who took the recipe for ice cream from China back to Italy?
5. When was ice cream first served in England?
6. Which king in England liked ice cream so much, he wanted it all for himself?

C **Answer each question in 2-3 sentences in your notebook.** **3 x 3 = 9 marks**

1. How is ice cream made these days?
2. What is said about Akbar's fondness for ice cream?
3. How did Ms Nancy Johnson make the process of making ice cream easier?

Coursebook comprehension

15 marks

A **Fill in the blanks with the correct words.** **8 x 1 = 8 marks**

1. In 'Abdullah and His Greed', the magic powder makes Abdullah b________.
2. In 'The Adventures of Sindbad the Sailor', Sindbad falls asleep on a w________.
3. In 'The Backwards Bob Rap', Backwards Bob addresses Aunt Pam as Aunt M________.
4. When Sindbad falls into the sea, he is saved by a floating b________.
5. In 'The Three Butterflies', the three brothers s________ each other.
6. In 'Caterpillar', the brown and f________ caterpillar is in a hurry.
7. In 'The Red Flower', the f________ comes up with a solution.
8. In 'Who Did Patrick's Homework?' an e________ helps Patrick with his homework.

B **In *Backwards Bob Rap*, Backwards Bob says names backwards. Can you think of three words that remain the same when read backward or forward?** **3 × 1 = 3 marks**

1. ____________ 2. ____________ 3. ____________

C **In *Who Did Patrick's Homework*, do you think Patrick was being dishonest by taking the help of the elf to do his homework? Give three reasons for your answer.** **4 marks**

____

____

____

____

____

____

____

____

15 marks

Grammar

Follow the instructions in brackets to answer the questions.

15 x 1 = 15 marks

1. I can run a long distance, but I ____________ run very fast.
   (Fill in the blank with 'must not' *or* 'can't'.*)*

2. I've only got one door key so you ____________ lose it!
   (Fill in the blank with 'must not' *or* 'can't'.*)*

3. My sister is three years ____________ than me.
   (Fill in the blank with the comparative form of 'old'.*)*

4. This room is __________ than that.
   (Fill in the blank with the comparative form of 'cold'.*)*

5. Would you like coffee __________ tea?
   (Fill in the blank with 'but' *or* 'or'.*)*

6. We could go swimming *but/or* we could go to the cinema.
   (Choose the correct word.)

7. He wrote his name very ______________.
   (Fill in the blank with the adverb of manner formed from 'careful'.*)*

8. She speaks very ______________.
   (Fill in the blank with the adverb formed from 'soft'.*)*

9. It's not heavy. I ______________ easily lift it.
   (Fill in the blank with 'can' *or* 'must'.*)*

10. It's dark in here and I __________ see anything.
    (Fill in the blank with 'must not' *or* 'can't'.*)*

11. Your bedroom is *clean/cleaner/cleanest* than mine.
    (Circle the correct word.)

12. Mira is tall *and/or* pretty.
    (Circle the correct word.)

13. don't forget/that letter to/to give/your teacher
    (Put the words in the correct order to make a polite command.)

14. please could/post this letter/you
    (Put the words in the correct order to make a polite command.)

15. light/please/switch on/the.
    (Put the words in correct order to make a polite command.)

15 marks

Writing

A **Think of all the stories you have read or films that you have seen that involved magic and adventure. Choose one of those stories and write it here as simply as you can. You may use the words given in the box.**

8 marks

disappear	find	lamp	lose	magical	mysterious	poor
power	promise	return	rich	search	set off	
strange	treasure	voyage				

Now draw a picture to go with your story.

B **Write a paragraph about any story character that you like best. You can use the following phrases.** **7 marks**

my favourite character — different from other characters — his/her good qualities — very likeable